# How Trees Must Feel

*My long two-pointed ladder's sticking through a tree*
*Toward heaven still. . . .*
　　　　　—Robert Frost

# How Trees Must Feel
## A Poetry Collection

## Chris Longenecker

**DreamSeeker Books**
**TELFORD, PENNSYLVANIA**

*an imprint of*
Cascadia Publishing House LLC

**Cascadia Publishing House orders, information, reprint permissions:**
contact@CascadiaPublishingHouse.com
1-215-723-9125
126 Klingerman Road, Telford PA 18969
www.CascadiaPublishingHouse.com

*How Trees Must Feel*
DreamSeeker Books is an imprint of Cascadia Publishing House LLC
Library of Congress Catalog Number: 2011013164
**ISBN 13:** 978-1-931038-87-4; **ISBN 10:** 1-931038-87-2
Book design by Cascadia Publishing House
Cover design by Gwen M. Stamm and inspired by a Pyramidal Beech at the
Louise Arnold Tanger Arboretum on the grounds of Lancasterhistory.org in
Lancaster, Pennsylvania.

The paper used in this publication is recycled and meets the
minimum requirements of American National Standard for Information
Sciences—Permanence of Paper for Printed Library Materials, ANSI Z39.48-1984.1984

Versions of poems in this collection have appeared in various outlets:
Some Bible quotations are paraphrases from the *King James Version* and the *New
Revised Standard Version*. A direct quote from KJV appears on p. 53.
The quote by Robert Frost on page 2 is an excerpt from "After Apple-Picking,"
from the book, *The Poetry of Robert Frost*, edited by Edward Connery Lathem.
Copyright 1969 by Henry Holt and Company, LLC. Reprinted by permission
of Henry Holt and Company.

**Library of Congress Cataloguing-in-Publication Data**
Longenecker, Chris, 1960-
How trees must feel : a poetry collection / Chris Longenecker.
    p. cm.
    Summary: "Aiming to write for these who tell her "I don't like poetry, but I
like what you write," Longenecker aims to create poems that are textually acces-
sible and often traditional in form yet (as her title poem signals) use the ordi-
nary to convey the extraordinary." "[summary]"--Provided by publisher.
    ISBN-13: 978-1-931038-87-4 (5.5 x 8.5 trade pbk. : alk. paper)
    ISBN-10: 1-931038-87-2 (5.5 x 8.5 trade pbk. : alk. paper)
    I. Title.
PS3612.O5324H69 2011
811'.6--dc22
                              2011013164

18  17  16  15  14  13  12  11     10 9 8 7 6 5 4 3 2 1

*To Rick*

# CONTENTS

## Foreword

Alhough for its first two centuries the largest Mennonite community outside of Europe—found in Lancaster County, Pennsylvania—basked amid a legendary natural fertility, there was scanty linguistic harvest. Verbosity was suspect. A mother tongue was given up. Aesthetics was for "the world." Excellence went into fecundity, food, faith and fellowship. Yet there is delightful evidence that seed of nuanced expression could be carried by this art-neutral ethos—in an imagination flavored but not limited by it—in the poems of Christine Longenecker, compassionate immigration counselor turned gardener.

Her unpretentious voice is startlingly imitative. Homage to Robert Frost unabashedly registered up front pervades the author's style, tone and themes. The effect is of a garrulous Yankee voice transposed into Lancaster County gossip. With an unassuming insouciance for accusations of imitation or obsoleteness of style, she can employ old-fashioned rhyme and meter in overtly Frostian wordplay over currents of contemporary seriousness.

The colloquial tone of course invites a reader's casual mood. Yet multiple layers of emotions emerge in re-readings, as a slant wryness turns quotidian images into moral metaphors.

It is not easy to write like this, not to speak of the fact that traditional rhyme-and-meter patterns are easily critiqued as anachronistic. (One sometimes suspects jealousy in the objections. Frost himself famously compared writing in free verse to playing tennis with the net down.)

In this poet's case, when unrhymed poems do appear, it is clear that it is not because she can't write otherwise. Her lapidary sonnets such as "This May be Madness, " "I Can Do This," "Not What You Might Think," or the love lyric, "If I

Die First" unfold here beautifully enough to illustrate why the genre is so enduring. On the other hand, an occasional break in taut metrics evoking Emily Dickinson's hymn stanzas reveals little fear of pedantic criticism.

The topographical and familial references in the Longenecker landscape can have a cheerfully domestic effect. Across the same scene, however, can flit shadows dark enough for the taste of readers with existential (if hopeful) anxiety. There is always emotional paradox. Beneath a wrapping of self-deprecating irreverence can lurk an offering of worship. An occasional expression that may jolt readers for whom a whole book is remembered for a single epithet will at the same time serve notice that this not a moral garden from which all the weeds have been pulled. All comes in that pleasantly undemanding conversational tone.

Finally, there is a constant interplay of lyric and narrative. The child's rhythm-and-rhyme in "Enlightened" playfully links the traditional Mennonite Sunday evening "children's meeting" with familial memories of verbal accidents. The boskily talkative "A Family Tree" offers as tender a vignette of trans-generational Lancaster County Mennonite life as has emerged from that three-century panorama. "How Trees Must Feel" parallels the author's ecstasy at getting a line, or a poem, just right. With her nerves running out along the branches into twigs and leaves, "Kindred Spirits" further evokes the mystique of poesis. "Some Outside Help" is a modest confession of faith. "Tree-Flung Seed" could appropriately be read at a wedding ceremony.

In today's congested forest, it is a pleasure to enter a clearing with this friendly arborist of words.

—*John L. Ruth, Author,* The Earth Is the Lord's:
A Narrative History of Lancaster Mennonite Conference
*Harleysville, Pennsylvania*

# All We with Branches

## How Trees Must Feel

I think I finally know how trees must feel
Who after years of floating seeds on hope
Land one, smack dab, in such a lap of mud
That the soft thud sends shudders of relief
Through every stem, each trembling petiole.
And all the clapping leaflets in the dome,
And all the vessels, xylem, ray and phloem,
Must feel the thrill from root to canopy
Of having landed one nut perfectly!

## Just Another Season

We wait together patiently
The barren winter trees and me.
We seldom speak, we never pace.
We simply bear the cold's embrace

And keep our worries to ourselves.
Why publish them? Not even elves
Can give a satisfying reason
Why winter has to be a season.

We know there's nothing to be done,
No one to call, no telephone.
And even were a number given,
Who'd answer for the when of heaven?

No one we know. No one we trust.
And so it's left to none but us
To watch the day's slow lengthening
The incremental inch of spring.

You might remark with what firm grace
We meet each morning's frozen face
Or how at dusk we watch dark fall
As if night didn't hurt at all.

It's not that we are not involved,
Committed, at the root resolved.
The cause of keeping love alive
Is ours. We're clear. Love will survive.

But sometimes love is kept inside
Far better than when published wide.
Sometimes they serve each other best
Who give their protestations rest,

Let feelings cool. If heartwood dies
It's part of growing up and wise.
Come spring we will be better fit
To meet it than the younger set.

For spring is not an easy lover.
And though he promises to flower
He sometimes breaks us with a storm
Before he shows he can be warm.

If we let be, don't make a fuss,
Perhaps the storm won't level us,
Won't break our hearts to make a point,
Won't twist our feelings out of joint.

And when he finally says, "I'm here
At last, my darling, have no fear,"
We'll hardly fling our branches wide
Shout out aloud, rush to his side.

Not likely. No. We'll hold our ground.
We'll look him over up and down.
We'll let him feel our silent stare.
We'll take our time in getting there.

Then quite politely we'll inquire,
Before he sets our hearts on fire,
Because, you see, we need to know:
"Will you stay then, or must you go?"

For staying is the only thing
That turns a winter thaw to spring.
And nothing—no, not God above
Nor anything earth's yet thought of,
Red breasted robin, turtledove—
But this makes loving into love.

## A Family Tree

I am the tree that bears the amber pears
Down the long lane next to the empty house
That stares at where there used to be a barn
And bears its absence like a widowed spouse.

I am the tree, the Kieffer canning pear.
My fruit, selected sweet, was bred to last,
To line the cellars of the coming year
For when the future hungers for the past.

I am the tree that sees the end of things.
Why I am left to see it, I don't know.
A few come down the lane to watch with me
But not as many as the years would owe.

We talk about it sometimes. The pecan
Has seen it from a slightly different angle.
She saw it from the side door, I the front.
Together we saw things we can't untangle.

And out in back the bittersweet saw things
That neither of us saw. When Papa died,
She saw the way the cattle tiptoed near
And kissed his forehead. She says they even cried.

I don't believe the cows cried actually.
Cows just look sad; that's just the way cows look.
As long as they have grass though, they don't mind
What else the good Lord gave or who he took.

Why Papa went to check on them at all
So late that night I never understood.
Maybe he felt a restlessness like theirs
And thought he'd try to settle what he could.

The only thing he settled though that night
Was his own heart. It never rose again.
That is, until his grandsons found him there
And bore him home, up the back steps, and then

They laid him finally in the living room.
Living was all they asked of him that night.
And he'd have given it them, I know he would,
If it had been a thing within his might.

"Now let's not lose our grip here," he'd have said.
"I'll be all right. Mama, let go my hand.
You're hurting me." And then she would have cried,
Relieved at what she now wouldn't have to stand.

And yet she would so stand it—eighteen years.
She was as strong as he was, every bit.
I remember the first time I realized her strength.
I overheard more than encountered it.

They were all standing by the kitchen door,
Papa and Cousin Henry, Papa's cousin,
And Mama and Marty, their oldest son, and Dan . . .
He may have been there, but I think he wasn't.

The argument was on the type of meat
Or how much salt to use in making souse—
Or was it scrapple? My memory's not clear.
I only know the tension in the house

Went well beyond the kitchen door that day.
All we with branches felt it to the pith.
It wasn't fists or even angry words
But innuendoes they were fighting with.

Papa said, "Look, our recipe is fine.
It don't need change. Leave well enough alone.
Course Henry thinks he has to interfere.
It's in his genes. I guess I should have known."

Now Henry clearly had a thing to say.
I heard the intake of his breath, the hiss.
But Marty, bless his heart for one so young,
Said, "Pop, please leave Aunt Reenie out of this."

Aunt Reenie was the source of the said genes.
She was Pop's aunt and Cousin Henry's mother.
She's also nearly married Pop's pop once
But then had gone and married his younger brother,

Henry's father. You see the way it was.
Not only tender feelings run so true
Between the generations like a thread,
But the taught cords of jealousy run too.

19 . . .

And Papa, like a boy at tug o' war,
Bore down, dug in, and gave it all his weight.
"Don't talk so dumb! That's dumb talk!"
He declared, the end of every argument to date.

And would have been the end of this one too.
That cord was thick and heavy as spun lead
And tore more than his fingers, Mama knew.
"Papa, you know he's right," was all she said.

I don't remember what the outcome was
In terms of scrapple recipes or souse,
And I'm not saying it was the last time
There was that kind of tension in the house,

But Papa listened. Henry listened too.
Their silence wasn't—but it seemed—so long.
My sympathies were everywhere at once.
Which way is harder, to be right or wrong?

Then someone broke the tension with a cough,
Said, "Milking time," and pushed aside a chair.
I heard Pop say as he went out the door,
"Where'd she get so wise?" as if it wasn't fair.

Ah, what a memory. What a family. And,
No pun intended, what a family tree.
I swear if I'd have loved them any more
They would have had to take an ax to me!

But they're all gone now. Died or moved away.
I miss their voices in the morning air,
The slamming of the doors, the barking dogs,
The tall ones reaching up to pluck a pear.

Sometimes I think I feel the tugging still,
Like phantom pains, I guess, with amputees.
The cherry says accept it, there's no cure,
That's just the way it is with family trees

And that I'll love again. I'll love again.
I say it to myself, but I confess
I dread the renovations in the house.
I'd almost rather bear the emptiness.

## Tree-Flung Seed

I found a tree-flung seed one autumn day,
Hard as a bone, black as a gleaming eye.
I tucked it in a crevice of my clothes
And "We shall see," I prob'ly thought or said.
How many semi-promises we make
And mean to keep; and this was one of those.

I had no more commitment to this seed, though,
Than to a thousand found on other trails
I'd meant to bury like a little kid
With promises to water every day.
If pockets had a tongue, they'd testify
How much I meant to do but never did.

So the tree that's growing now in my backyard
Is no more mine because of a seed I threw
Into an old clay pot and then forgot
Than you are mine because of a glance I threw
Across a room eleven years ago.
If only it were that simple, but it's not.

A promise isn't over once it's made
Anymore than seeds are trees just 'cause they've sprouted.
To bring a tender sapling to fruition
Takes something even Saint Paul failed to mention.
For after all abideth now *four* things.
It takes faith, hope and love *and* repetition.

Water and soil and sun—faith, hope and love—
Water and soil and sun through many a season.
The first three may get most of the attention,
But in the end it's mainly repetition
That grants us trees and anniversaries.
And that's at least worth honorable mention.

## Some Outside Help

Pale peach tree blossoms open very fast
And very sweet, but ill-advisedly.
Had they but asked a wiser tree or me,
We would have told them, "No, please wait. The last

Thing you should do is rush the opening.
Like stepping on the stage a beat too soon.
The house is ready, but they have to tune
The orchestra—each reed, each brass, each string.

Before you spring wait longer in the dark.
The blacks will keep your bloom. Nothing is lost
By weighing eagerness against the cost
Of breaking out too soon. Even the lark

Knows singing must be timed. So must a flower.
There's nothing says a peach tree must be first.
Let cherries do that. Let their blossoms burst
And hold the rapturous audience in their power."

But will the branchlings listen to the wise
And place their blossoms firmly on the shelf?
No more than I will listen to myself
Or pluck the proverbial plank from my own eyes.

No, flowers will bloom exactly when they will
And if we care for them at all—at all,
We'll do as farmer's do. You may recall
Last winter when they said the cold would kill,

All farmers who had peaches, bless their souls,
Got out their hoses, did what God would not.
(Or, bless his soul, perhaps he just forgot.
I'm sure he has a thousand other goals

More meet than freezing peaches—or I hope
He does at least.)  In any case the trees
Were left to farmers who in dungarees
And high-top boots (the vestments of a Pope

Could not have been more suitable attire)
Eyes raised toward heaven, aimed their weapons, prayed
(The temperature was falling as they sprayed)
And met the raging winter's fire with fire!

Or should I say they met its ice with ice?
The water wrapped each little bud and froze.
Each little beating heartbeat, though it rose,
Could not break through that little fisted vice.

And well it was they couldn't, for the sun
Was all that they had seen; you can't see cold.
And what they had not seen had made them bold.
So bold, I think, they would have been undone

Had not some sleepy farmer in this case
Reached out a hand and dared to interfere
Beyond his genus, species, even sphere,
And been a credit to the human race

By saving peaches. Now I may be wrong.
I'm not promoting human intervention
Without a deal of healthy apprehension.
God knows we meddle where we don't belong.

But sometimes—even though I almost hate
To say it—some outside help is good
And might prevent some heartache. If I could
I'd trust a peach tree farmer with my fate.

For wouldn't it be nice if like a tree
Somebody with a hose looked out for us?
I know our seasons aren't analogous.
The need is though, as far as I can see.

## Too Much of a Good Thing

There are too many apples in our back yard.
Two kinds of Delicious . . . the third one's hard
To say, but I think it's a Macintosh.
They're delicious too, but oh my gosh,

There are too many apples! They fall and rot.
And I'm not just talking one rotten spot,
I'm talking whole apples. They're going to waste.
I do what I can, but in spite of my haste

To turn them into pies or schnitz,
Three quarters go bad or get nibbled to bits
By rabbits and yellow jackets and ants.
It's as if a traditional worm had no chance,

Not to mention a person. I wonder if God
Ever thinks about waste or just blows his whole wad
Every time, like a gambler with no self-restraint.
I mean apples are good; this is not a complaint

About apples or even a justification
Of what I'm about to do. No explanation
Could justify that, no penance absolve.
I can't believe I of all people would solve

Anything with an ax! But before buds get fat,
We have to do something because after that
It's too late. Yes, I know, we could give more away,
But they're not very pretty. It's not like we spray

Every ten days all season. I mean who has the time,
The equipment, the know-how? Though my husband says I'm
Kind of cute on a ladder and might have a knack
For the loftier parts. Still it's *time* that we lack.

What we have in abundance are apples times three.
We're like parents of triplets or pirates at sea
With too heavy a treasure. Will we make it to land
Or just sink where we are with the spoils in our hand,

Our last frantic wave a bizarre pantomime
Of too many apples and not enough time?

# Toward Heaven

## For Balance

The lily on my sill for sheer desire
Inclines each day a little to the sun.
She tips her chin to that forbidden fire,
By sweet degrees a little nearer won.
If I, like she, could grow toward what I love,
Lean toward what I would lean, could really see,
Finally, beyond this frame, what shines above
In unalloyed desirability,
I would! But something turns me back each day
An inch or two for balance, pot and all,
Away from what I love. Come eyes, away.
I dare not see nor focus nor recall.
For if I should, God knows, earth's ledge is thin.
I'd lean so far toward heaven, I'd fall in.

## Loon Landing

Some say the soul's born walking
And needs God's help to fly
Away from the teeming intimate earth
Into the boundless sky.

I say the soul's born flying
And needs God's help to land
And every ounce of Providence
To waddle a world of sand.

## Lion or Lamb

If I am conquered, it will not be
Because I chose to come.
God should have known he couldn't have
This one a lamb.

He'll have me as a lioness,
Exhausted if at all;
Collapsed behind the eyes and bloody
He'll have to drag me home.

## Learning to Crawl

My lips are too thick to savor
The tiny sweet flavor of dew;

My feet too well-booted to bleed
For the wee wicked scalpel of thistle.

I must learn like the snail in the grass
Slowly for hours and small, to crawl.

## A Refrain

Last night I heard a sweet refrain.
As near as I could ascertain,
It was a thought complete with words,
Inflection, innuendo birds
Would understand. But I was struck
Not by the meaning but the pluck
Of speaking out so loud so late.
What sorts of birds communicate
So late at night? This was no owl,
No nightingale, no barnyard fowl,
Though they've been known to be mistaken
About the hour and to awaken
Whole farms at two and three o'clock.
No, this was something with less cock,
Less listen up, less look at me.
It almost sounded like a plea.
I wonder if it even thought
A soul was listening. Prob'ly not.

Sometimes at night when we're alone,
Or think we are, we might be prone
To say a thing out verbally
With passion or hyperbole
We'd never dare by light of day,
Or if we did, we'd know we'd pay.
Thank God for God who doesn't count
On words alone, though they amount
To great objections or oblations
About our lot or all creation's.

Whether we lay our prayers on thin
Or thick, God surely takes them in
With that same cosmic grain of salt.
God is the word. It's not God's fault
He takes our prayers less literally
Than we so earnest ritually
Take him—or her. There's one right there.
A word for God beyond compare.
There are those who'd rather go to war
Than take *him* as a metaphor.

We say "He speaks," but most agree
The voice is still and small and we
Hear it (even those who claim to hear)
With something other than the ear.
Forgive me, John, if I explore
The limits of your metaphor.
But as I lay there late last night
Willing that bird with all my might
To speak again that I might claim
I'd heard such-and-so bird by name
On Tuesday night at half past ten
So I could go to sleep again
And waking never once recall
That I'd heard anything at all,
It didn't speak. It held its own.
And here is where I should have known
What took me next to dawn to see.
This bird was not reflecting me
And my small prayers. This may sound odd.
This bird, I swear, reflected God.

Not the word of God that any quack
Can claim to quote but the holding back,
The stopping short and holding steady,
The I have said enough already.
Isn't it strange the way we plead
For more when what we really need
Is to hold still and pay attention
To what God hasn't failed to mention?
Although God can, of course, speak bird
Quite fluently and wind and word
And rain in several dialects,
Sometimes it's as if he elects
To hold his thoughts (or hers) in spaces
Between the birds and other places,
As if not just awake but sleeping,
Not just in giving but in keeping,
He'd done enough; it'd be alright.
At least that's what I got last night.

## By a Different Road

When I take Route 441 to work
In lieu of faster more efficient routes,
I feel as though I'm going somewhere else
Or even that I might be someone else,
Like a woman I met once in a waiting room
With a bevy of freckled children waiting for shots.
They were from here, near the river, maybe Bainbridge.
All but the youngest one went in alone
And came back proudly brandishing an arm.
The speckled sycamore born by the water has arms like that.
She had them too, a mother's muscled arms,
The kind of arms that pick you up at night
And carry you in from the car when you're asleep.
I've been on the receiving end of those
But never on the lifting, unless you count
The lifting down of furniture from a truck
And up a thousand thousand flights of stairs
To furnish countless rooms for refugees.
We social workers are a kind of mother,
But not the kind that lives down by the water
And raises children purely for the pleasure,
Or so I can imagine if I want to.
I even have a trailer all picked out
With a rusty car beside it and a boat,
A boat that hooks the river like a comma
For me to rest my mind on every time.
And where I go, or where I let it take me,
All up and down the wet, wide Susquehanna,
Wild and serene and everything between,

I couldn't even tell you if I had to.
I only know it's not where I'm supposed to.
I don't condone going where you're not supposed to,
But going not where you're supposed to go's
A different joy. And I do recommend it.
As long as you get there eventually,
Just by a different road and on your own time,
The way some people get to church or even . . .
(Or even, I was going to say to heaven,
But that, I guess, would be another poem.)
I see no harm and maybe an advantage.
You may be late, but you get better mileage.

# Souls Crossing

## The Alva

The waitress' name was Bobby.
She had a bitter edge.
Although she'd bring you coffee
And your biweekly wedge

Of cream cheese with a bagel,
She wouldn't deign to show
That she was glad to see you.
She'd call you honey though.

"Here's your coffee, honey,"
She'd say with lip up-curled
And fling the napkin after like a
Gauntlet at the world.

Her manners were deplorable.
She'd win no charm award.
But if you said, "One egg today,"
She knew one over hard

With wheat toast and no butter,
With water and no ice.
Why waste your time on manners
When memory will suffice?

Not that I criticize or care.
I'd rather be ignored
At that hour in the morning,
Provided coffee's poured.

So when she asked one day, "Whatever
Happened to the man
Who used to ride the train with you?"
She had to ask again.

"You know the man who took the train,
Gray beard and dignified?
He used to come in here with you."
I nodded, but I lied.

I had no memory of the man,
And if he took the train,
It hadn't made impression yet
On my myopic brain.

Sometimes I get the feeling that
I haven't been all there,
Like along with my umbrella I've
Misplaced my brain somewhere—

Maybe on the overhead rack or
Somewhere at the station —
I wonder if their lost and found
Has brain refrigeration.

But Bobby wasn't interested
In where my brain had been.
She prob'ly wondered how a girl
Could miss an entire man.

So I promised her I'd find him. Seemed
The least that I could do.
Besides the way she feigned indifference
Seemed to dare me to.

So I spoke with every bearded man
Even halfway dignified.
And even that criterion
I finally set aside.

But no one knew of Bobby of
The Alva Restaurant
Or claimed to have been served by her
His daily egg croissant.

I thought she'd let me off the hook.
It took her weeks to say
What each knew each was thinking:
"Looks like he went away."

Months passed. Then Bobby went away.
The other waitress said
That she'd been fired. My eyes inquired.
She simply shook her head.

I let it go. But then one day
A hand clamped on my shoulder
With "I'm your man." I stammered, "Could
You be a little bolder?"

And then I realized who he was—
The beard, the dignified—
Well, not exactly either, but
I saw it if I tried.

I took him to the manager
Lest Bobby's ghost should plague us.
But he just waved us jocosely,
"She married and moved to Vegas."

I wish that I could say that I
Had stopped him then and there,
Said, "Wait, don't lie to us. We know
You fired her. We're aware

That no one moved to Vegas much
Less married anyone!"
But I didn't realize that he
Had lied till he was gone.

I don't know why it mattered, why
I didn't let it go, why I
Had to find that waitress, had
To let that strange man know.

The comings and the goings of
The soul are so mundane,
So casual its crossings, such
Unimportant pain.

And Bobby and the stranger,
The manager and me
Are the heroines and heroes of
This vast vulgarity.

Not the stuff of Leer or Hamlet
Or, say, Beauty and the Beast.
But you have to give us credit for
A parody at least.

We're at least as universal. And you'll
Hear that same sweet plea
From our low and holy darkness
If you lean . . . *remember me.*

## This May Be Madness

I pulled my car into a Mobil station,
And who should come to pump my gas for me,
But Don Quixote. Out of all creation,
A place I'd least expected chivalry.
He bowed, "I'll pump your gas, my lady fair."
To my surprise, I curtsied perfectly.
Now I'm no lady, but I'd almost swear
I gave my hand like I was meant to be.
He held my trembling fingers to his lips.
I can still see us in the side view mirror.
And I still feel the curtsy in my hips
As tangible as Jacob's souvenir.
A dislocated hip was how he knew
Which dreams are fantasy and which are true.

## A Dry Summer

Down at the county park a mile from town
Two hundred rented garden plots in rows
Lay baking in the hot midsummer sun.
Two gardeners from the city, pale and young,
Stood leaning on their shovels, having begun
This project to get back in touch with God
By way of earth. Or that was what they thought
When they had started. Now they only clung
Onto their shovels, waiting for something gone
To seep back in like water up the roots
Of plants that they were tending. Neither spoke.
After about a minute, Peter moved,
Picked up his spade and struck it down again,
As if to make some point by that alone.

"Well, standing here won't make it rain," he said.
"We might as well get back to work again."

Then Dee Dee, moving like a waking thing
And blinking, rubbed her forehead with her hand.
She didn't pick her shovel up. Instead
She stooped and picked a hardened piece of dirt
Up from the earth. Then where she knelt she rubbed
It in her hand till she had rubbed it mostly
Into sand. Then with the little stone heart
That remained, she stood and turning to Peter

Softly said, "There's nothing exactly gentle
About the land or about farming, nothing
So kind or mild. I don't know where I got
That impression as a child."

                              He leaned a little
Toward her and he smiled. "Unless it was
Your grandpa. He was kind. And Mexican farmers
Here have been mild and kind too for the most part."

"Well it isn't the land that makes them kind.
At least I can't imagine how it would.
It's so damn hard, like now, and stupid rain
Never coming. It doesn't make me kind."

"Maybe it will, you work it long enough."

"I work myself to death and I'm a saint.
Is that it?"
                    "Saint Dee Dee?  Possibly.

Look, Maybe it doesn't make them kind so much
As wears them kind like plowing wears their hands."

She dropped the stone before she answered him.
"I know. I fingerprinted farmers. Was it
Just last year when they were getting legal?
I thought at first my ink pad had gone bad.
But it's their fingers. Fingers of old farmers
Are smooth as pebbles worn from running water
Till they have no more ridges left to print from

Than pebbles have. It's like the earth had worn
The nap off. I found it sad or something
I don't know. I'd want to hold their old worn
Hands a bit too long sometimes."

                              "You would.
I can just see you holding old men's hands."

"And women's! They were just the same as men's.
All hands were worn out, threadbare at the ends."

He winked at her. "I'm sure they were," he said.
"Here show me how you held those farmer's hands."

He offered her both hands expectantly.
She took his hands but held them absently,
Not looking at them, looking at the weeds,
As if she were a seer and had seen
(Or was about to see, had nearly seen)
Some answer to the hardness of the land
In something there that could be read like tea
Leaves if one dared. She clung to him for anchor
And she stared. "What I don't get . . . what I
Don't understand, Pete, is how these farmers go on
Farming every year and how they keep
Believing, knowing what they do, in God,
Much less some God of everlasting kindness.
I couldn't Pete, and that's the truth. Could you?"

"Believe in God? Of course I could. I do.
And you. You'll be surprised how you'll believe

In God again come rain."

                         "Oh no, not me.
No. I'll believe in rain again come rain.
Not God. If I'd believe in God, I'd be
Ashamed. Believing in God only when
There's rain? What kind of faith is that?"

"The going kind, I fear."

                         "Not mine, I swear!"


"Aw, Dee, relax, you're too sincere. Look here.
Remember the flowers of the field. . . ."

                                    "No you
Look, Pete. The land's not kind. Why should we think
That God is?
              Whoever it was that said
'Look at the lilies; see how they neither toil
Nor spin, our heavenly Father feeds them'
Was either kidding or just wishful thinking.
It wasn't any farmer said that surely."

"O ye of little faith. I love you dearly,
But there are other flowers besides the lily.
Look at this weed—I don't recall the name—
It withers. Like your faith, it fades away.
But give it half a drop of rain, it's back
Blooming its little heart out for the world

As if it never doubted for a second
Rain would come. That's how folks are with God too,
Even you. You'll see. Our souls shrink in
To wait for God the way the plasmalemma
In the leaves shrinks in to wait for rain.
Lucky for you, your soul is made that way."

"Lucky for me?" she whispered, turning away.
But the corners of her mouth were beginning to play
And she winked at the weeds before she turned his way.
"Lucky for me? Damn lucky for God, I'd say."

### Enlightened

Russell was a preacher preaching
From his pulpit in the air,
And the people trembled in their pews
At the things he said from there.

All about the straight and narrow,
All about the sins of youth;
And the way he waved his Bible
Well, you knew it was the truth.

Little Willie bit his fingers.
Little Rachel chewed her hair.
Neither one could look at Russell,
Brother Russell, Russell Baer.

And he even made up stories
Full of creatures, vile, depraved,
Meant to frighten little children
Till their wicked souls were saved.

One time in the dead of winter,
In an evening service too,
He was telling such a story
And his eyes were steely blue.

Knees were clenched along the benches,
Lips were parted, breath was thin.
Russell wasn't God incarnate,
But he might as well have been.

He had everyone believing
That the world was one dark wood,
And each soul was ripe for ambush
Like a blithe Red Ridinghood

Skipping lightly through the forest
Unafraid and unaware
Of the danger in the darkness
Of the evil lurking there.

Willie's heart was in his stomach.
Rachel's heart was in her throat.
Russell's heart was in his story.
He was reaching the key note.

And he paused. This was his moment.
And I quote here Brother Baer:
"T'was a rustle in the bushes,
And the rustle was a bear!"

Then he growled just for good measure
And the congregation winced.
God was smiling from the heavens,
Brother Russell was convinced.

And the whispers from his victims,
"Psst. . . . Our Russell is a bear!"
And the stifled little giggles
He assumed were sounds of prayer.

Now you mustn't think that Russell
Was a stupid man or slow.
God has blinded greater leaders
For his purposes, you know.

And there's sure no greater purpose
Than a well-positioned pun.
And this homonym was heaven-
Sent if ever there was one.

Still the people they tried not to
Laugh. They knew it wasn't good.
But you know how when you try
Not to, it's worse than if you would?

So they bit their lips and chewed
Their cheeks and looked down at the floor
But as much as they tried not to
Laugh, they shook the benches more.

Then God did the strangest thing,
I think, the gods have ever done.
He allowed his man to get it,
Not to sweat it, to have fun!

Then the entire congregation
Laughed till they could hardly stand it.
And the one who laughed the loudest
Was the Russell who began it.

Now I wouldn't go so far's
To say salvation came that day,
But that some went home enlightened
I believe it's safe to say.

And now when it seems that evil
Is around you everywhere,
Remember how God sent the pun
To save you from *the bear*.

## Tidal Spring

We saw his light before he heard our knock.
The dog's head cocked but opted not to bark.
So many noises happen in the dark;
No point in giving the old man a shock.

He looked like Vermeer's lady in the light,
Yet with that bowl of popcorn on his knee
More like a Norman Rockwell actually,
Like a self-portrait of the old man might.

This was no painting, though, but real repose.
I wondered if we ought to go away.
But Dad was more inclined than I to stay
And less inclined to walk on tippy-toes

Around old men. He tried a knock again
Then felt the knob and found it wasn't locked
(Don't ask me why he'd ever even knocked)
And let himself, and me included, in.

There on the threshold like two thieves we stood
Having stolen silence from that April eve.
They gave it freely though; I half believe
They welcomed company, however rude,

The dog especially. Somehow she knew
That company meant chairs came off the couch.
You never saw so meaningful a crouch
As she assumed after a bark or two

From which she leapt, the moment the chairs were off,
Onto the couch in half a second flat.
Dad didn't even see her till he sat.
The old man hid his smile behind a cough

Then shooed her gently down. We visited.
We told him where we'd been all afternoon,
Out in his pasture, out where they say the moon
That pulls the very ocean from its bed

Looks down and lifts a certain pasture spring
Out of itself, out of the very ground,
Then puts it back again. Of course they've found
(Those scientists who study everything)

The moon has nothing to do with the spring at all.
It's just some natural siphon mechanism
That causes an apparent synchronism
Between the tides and the spring's rise and fall.

We call it Tidal Spring though anyway
And hold our vigil once or twice a year
To watch it rise and flow . . . and disappear
Or disappoint us like it did today.

"It's been too dry," Isaiah Pearlman said.
(That was his name.) "It's been too dry too long.
The cows, they know it too; they're never wrong.
You won't find cattle in a dry streambed

Lookin' for miracles." "But they were there,"
I countered doubtfully. "That was for you.
Cows have to check out anything that's new.
A reverend and a pretty face are rare

This side of Broadway." And then he winked at Dad.
But it was such an old man thing to do
I couldn't take offense. Besides it's true.
Every time we go there it's as if we had

A congregation, devotees, all cows.
They follow us, sometimes even at a run.
I'd never go alone. With Dad it's fun.
He runs back at them, slaps them like old pals.

"Hello there, Polly, Dolly . . ." any name;
And every word he says to them they mark
As though enthralled. This day they formed an arc,
A perfect semicircle. Who could blame

A simple pastor and a farmer's son
For doing what came naturally when faced
With such a perfect audience? He based
His thoughts on chapter forty-one

Of Genesis and preached about the kine
Who in a dream one night came to a king
And how it changed the course of everything.
His inspiration, though less than divine,

Was more than many sermons I've endured.
No cow looked bored. Isaiah from his chair
Said afterward that he wished he'd been there
To see their faces. "Old men can't afford

To miss good sermons even if they are
Out in a field full of mud and manure.
Sometimes you have to wade through shit before
You find whatever it is your guiding star

Is leading toward." This last seemed to be said
For the benefit of a woman who that minute
Had opened the kitchen door and now stood in it.
She smiled with half her mouth as if a thread

Had pulled it from behind and then let go.
Again like thieves I felt that we intruded,
This time on pain, but again we were included.
A visit has it's own internal flow,

Like Tidal Spring. And whatever it lets you see
Or lets you know isn't always up to you.
It helps though if you stay an hour or two,
The minimum for giving mystery

A chance to turn the surface soil wet.
And if you're patient, you may even find out
If she is daughter, niece, in-law or out
And what that smile is all about. I bet

You're wondering if we did. But truth be known,
Although we stayed an hour, maybe more,
She didn't talk that much. We got a tour,
Though, of the house. Turned out they didn't own

But only rented it, which I guess defined
Them too as visitors. And in a way
We all are visitors, the sages say.
Before we left, he told me where to find

The purple lady's slipper in the wood.
I told him where to find it in a poem.
And then we shook their hands and headed home
Where Mom was wondering if we ever would.

## A Little to the Left or Right

If they had rendezvoused when they were young
They might have been more cavalier in love.
He might have been more dashing, she more suave.
What witty repartee they might have flung
Over their champagne glasses all night long
And never even felt one awkward pause.
But he was maybe fifty, fifty-one
And she was thirty-eight. I know because
I was the woman, I was the one who was
Poised to a point, but like a bow taut drawn
(Arm bent and trembling, heart bent with holding my own)
I was past witty and light years beyond cavalier.
Had I been aiming at a fox or deer,
Had he a ten point rack that raked the skies,
I might have hit him right between the eyes
And hauled him home, a trophy on a bier.
But if age has taught me anything, it's this:
Don't aim directly at your heart's desire,
A little to the left or right of bliss
Is better lest you prove like Artemis
So focused that you miss the obvious—
Your lover may be in your line of fire.
Don't shoot! That is, unless you aim to miss.

**Turtle Rock**

There once were some turtles lined up on a log
Side by side, 'bout an inch between each.
They were sunning, as terrapins do in a bog,
Barely conscious like girls on the beach.

Oblivious really to anything but
The hot sun and the good will it bore them.
Their necks were outstretched and their eyelids were shut
As if whatever ailed heat would cure them.

They were hardly prepared then for what would ensue,
Nor did I have the least premonition.
There was only one other small turtle in view
Not exactly arousing suspicion.

For as is the case among reptile and human
When an enemy comes from within
You're hardly aware that the danger is loomin'
Till it's practically under your skin.

This small turtle now had but one intention
For which there was but one solution.
She wanted to join that beach turtle convention.
Which was going to require revolution.

Not a terrorist plot or a bloody revolt
Or a mutineer mounting a coup,
But a simple reversal, a child's summersault,
Also known as the old switcheroo.

It's the first rule they teach you in turtle pre-school—
Taking turns in the unit on sharing.
But when turtles who have don't remember the rule
The have-nots must be that much more daring.

This one's focus, then, first was to get a firm grip
For what might be a wobbly ascent.
Like me she was probably biting her lip,
If she had one, for she was hell-bent

On not slipping. And the gripping was starting to smart
And her muscles were starting to swell.
The front ones, that is. The back were, for their part,
Flapping practically out of their shell!

And then for a moment she hung by one arm
And I thought she was going to totter,
But she had to reach higher, and that proved the charm
To get her butt out of the water.

And all would have been well, and all would have been fine
Had she weighed just a little bit less.
She would have just taken her place in the line,
One turtle more crowded, I guess.

But she weighed what she did (or her derrière did),
And once it was no longer buoyed,
The log shifted and suddenly every eyelid
Every muscle and wit was employed

In an instinctive—whoa—counter-balancing shift
To restore the slant sun to its place
In the sky—whoops—and then some, if you get my drift.
"Easy there. Steady girl. About face!"

Shouted someone from starboard, or was it from port?
Hard to say when you're losing your balance.
For though lumberjacks may have made it a sport
Rolling logs isn't one of the talents

Of sunbathing turtles. They were tossed side to side
And their little bow legs couldn't master
The wide undulations of this wild water ride
Nor avoid the impending disaster.

Still for creatures you think of as having no speed,
Their maneuvers were quite animated.
And this river dance show, I have to concede,
Was as riveting as it was fated.

Till plip, plop, ploop, plup. That was all. It was done.
No encore, no sensationalism.
And the little she-turtle was now in the sun,
At least until her next baptism.

## A Bat Out of Contex

I saw an ash the other day
Go floating through the air
And then land flatly on a wall
As if it were pinned there
By wind, as I imagined,
But something made me pause
And look again and then I saw
The ash had little claws.

## Just A

It was just a chance encounter along the way.
Walking home we would have passed each other,
For I was walking faster than the other,
But for the dog. Let's call it a *pouffé*;

It wasn't what you think when you think of dog.
Sometimes it's better to invent a new word
Than to stretch a used one, even a tried and true word,
So far beyond its broadest analogue

To where it's barely recognizable,
Albeit in this case adorable
And not apparently ignorable
Though that may well have been advisable.

"My my, aren't you a cutie. What's your name?
Oh, yes, you like that, don't you, behind the ears
And on the belly welly! Have you no fears
Of what could happen to your dainty frame?

Don't worry. I won't hurt you. That's a good girl.
Or is it a boy? I can't always tell."
"It's a girl. Her name is C.J. She's not well.
I'm not so well myself. My head's a-whirl.

It's been a day from hell, a very bad day."
And to be sure, she did look rather bad.
It may have been the missing teeth she had
Or the bent back. Even a goddess may

Look less than well dealt such a hand of deuces.
"I'm sorry," I said finally after a pause.
"What happened?" I was hesitant because,
While their pain had primed my sympathetic juices,

I wasn't sure I cared to get involved.
"Well yesterday I knew she wasn't right.
So finally I called the vet last night.
If only . . . Ah, but things are never solved

By if, what if, if only . . . that's for sure.
Besides I couldn't make my husband go.
He's second shift. He needs his sleep, you know.
So we took the bus. I even called before

To make sure I could hold her on my lap.
They said no problem, and at first it wasn't.
But at the transfer this new driver doesn't
Believe me. Yep, starts to give me crap

About how permission has to be in writing!"
"You're kidding. Couldn't he see that you'd be stranded?"
"Of course he could.  But youth is heavy-handed
About the rules, and I didn't feel like fighting.

Not that I can't. I've fought for everything.
My health, my jobs, tenure, PhDs. . . .
Today though I was tired. I just said, 'Please
Call your supervisor. They said I could bring. . . '

And then he slammed the door right on my face!
You know, the folding kind? I couldn't believe it.
I rapped the glass with my cane, then tried to heave it
(You can imagine with what style and grace)

After the bus 'cause he was pulling away.
And when I went to fetch it, so help me,
I swear he backed the bus right into me!"
"My God! Are you alright? Are you OK?"

"Well, I was down and kind of in a daze.
It's amazing I didn't have one of my regular fits.
Seizures, I mean, not rage. I get them. It's
A condition I have. I'm used to them. C.J.'s

Used to them too. I used to warn my classes.
But they were great. They took it all in stride.
If I had one, they'd turn me on my side
Till it was over. Till those nosey asses

In administration got wind of things and said
I should have told them that I was disabled.
I wasn't, bless them, till they had me labeled.
So much for fair! Anyway from there I pled

My case out west. I'd heard of St. Ignatius.
I thought somehow the Jesuits might be . . . nicer.
But prejudice, no matter how you slice her,
Is still mean, I guess. But I'm being too loquacious,

And I should stop and give C. J. a drink.
We're almost there, girl. That's right, drink your fill.
We only have to climb this one last hill
And then you'll recognize the field, I think.

But you go on. No doubt you're homeward bound
And you'll be late. No need to wait for us.
I only told what happened at the bus
'Cause you're a listener. I'm not the first you've found

Who'll tell her story, am I? What do you do?
A journalist?" "No, just a secretary."
"Just a. . . . *Just A?* Now listen to me very
Closely. I'm going to tell you something true.

There's no such thing as *just a* anything!"
Her voice had turned remonstrative in tone.
So eager to enjoin, her features shone
With enthusiasm. Had she begun to sing

Like some bedraggled scarecrow out of Oz,
It hardly would have been a transformation
Less fitting with my growing expectation
Of who this wounded, toothless woman was

Who now was lecturing me on self-esteem.
"I didn't mean. . . . It just came out that way."
But nothing I could subsequently say
Would disavow the homiletic theme

I had unleashed. Once truth has been set free
It's mighty hard to get it back again
And even harder not to rub it in
Especially when it's true bilaterally.

But we were coming now upon the field
Where we must part, each to our separate place.
We exchanged first names, acknowledging a trace
Of what we'd shared. Neither willing to yield

A last name, though, or a complete address.
Our conversation now designed to fill
The last few hundred yards, mostly downhill.
We each assured the other one that, yes,

We would be fine, health and self-image wise.
And C.J., too, seemed fine, in fact so well
Straining toward home, her mistress nearly fell
Holding onto her, flinging her last good-byes

Into the air as if the twilight heard.
And as the stars emerged, there came a sound,
A tiny voice the distance nearly drowned.
"There's no such thing as *just a!*" her last word.

## Not What You Might Think

He let me see him naked. This was not
What you might think. This was no bedroom plot
With a hot mattress. We didn't kiss or touch.
I didn't even look at him that much.
His mother called. He brought the kitchen phone
Out to the porch so as not to be alone.
(I was having lunch. I don't know what I had.)
And listened to her talk about his dad
Who wasn't well. I heard him say, "I know."
Then a long pause and then again, "I know.
It's OK, Mom. She's crying," he said to me.
I must have raised my eyes in sympathy.
And then I saw. He didn't try to hide.
He let me see him naked as he cried.

### I Can Do This

I've mastered pain. I studied it in school.
And then I practiced, sometime hours a day.
I know how to negotiate the pull
Against the gut until it goes away.
And when it doesn't, I know how to wait,
To put a good face on it, or to cry
If it's too hard. And when it won't abate,
I've even mastered wishing I could die.
But joy has never tested me till now.
Oh, I've had blissful episodes, it's true,
But nothing that required learning how
To foster and sustain it until you.
So if at first I falter, don't be sad.
I'm sure I'll get the hang of being glad.

**Indecent Proposal**

I went to Brandywine to that museum
To see the paintings done by Andrew Wyeth.
They have the Helga series. You should see 'em
Why in the *Daydream* one, I swear she lieth
Like a lover in Elizabethan sonnet.
When I got home, I found my lover cleaning,
As naked as a bee without a bonnet,
And suddenly his buttock had new meaning.
"Honey," I said, "Would you pose nude for me
So I could paint you?" "What? Like this?" he said.
Then looking downward in self-scrutiny
And back at me, "I wouldn't be caught dead!
Some things, my dear, the world must never know.
The dustpan and the brush would have to go."

## Catching the Keystone Daily

They know my face if not my name
  yet hold the brakes for me.
It's like there's some magnetic force
  between the train and me.
Conductors smile and scratch their heads
  as I come clomping down
The metal stairs like Cinderella
  hitching up her gown.
The clock will strike, the whistle blow,
  the train will pull away,
But I'll be safely in my coach,
  barely, for one more day.

# Within the Realm

## Kindred Spirits

If I trust anything, I trust the weather.
Though to its terrors I am scarcely blind.
Still since our bloods pulse more or less together
By the same salts and liquids both confined,

I trust it. Not that it will never harm me
Or never charm me falsely and then change,
But rather that its ways, though they alarm me,
Are mainly in their magnitude and range

Different than my ways. We have our temperate zones
And our extremes, our poles and our equators.
And for expression we have sighs and groans.
We're neither of us great articulators.

Yet while I wrack my brains for rhymes with reasons,
I wrest some reassurance from the way
The weather wracks the skies and rhymes with seasons,
A kind of cosmic comfort you might say,

As though there were on some colossal level
Some sympathy for rhyming in the spheres
Some impulse to delight if not to revel
In rhythm. I can almost feel the years

Reeling in time, in seasons to the measure,
Not perfectly, of course, but there's a yearning
I recognize and then a sigh of pleasure
Upon some sweet theme's having turned returning.

**The Other Side of Death**

One shouldn't rake the leaves while they're still falling
Nor shovel snow while snow's still coming down.
It makes no sense to bail while skies are bawling.
There's something to be said for hunkering down
And waiting till the chaos has abated,
The worst well over and the damage done,
Then crawling from the safety where you've waited
To set things right beneath a gentler sun.
But sometimes we must fight even though we're losing
Against the current even though we'll drown,
And waiting safely isn't ours for choosing.
It's do or die and danger all around
Till finally when we've time to catch our breath,
We find we're on the other side of death.

## If I Die First

If I die first and you go on to live
A pleasant life yet miss me now and then,
Remember most that which I tried to give
And not my stingier moments if you can.
I'm counting on the tricks the memory plays
On those who grieve. The one who's gone seems dear
Beyond accounting. Why, in only days
It's like an angel had been living here.
I know I don't deserve it, but I'd try
To do the same for you if it were me.
Already when your death gets in my eye
It's all that I can do to even see
Past all the wings and halos, things so pure,
Your socks that are still lying on the floor.

## Enough's Enough

For ages men have pondered sacred questions
Like how many angels can dance on the head of a pin.
My own preoccupations have been less lofty
But no less concerned with the situation we're in.

When I was a little girl, I used to wonder
If I were standing naked at the North Pole,
Or only in my panties, how many blankets
Would it take to keep me warm and comfortable?

When I suggested five-hundred to Mommy,
She said, "That should be plenty," and so I slept.
Had the men with the angel question come to Mother
And had she applied her that-should-be-plenty precept,

I wonder if the sages would have rested,
Like me tucked in clear up to their bearded chins,
And in the morning barely remembered the question
Except that it had something to do with pins.

I wish all five-year-olds and theologians
And all who find themselves susceptible
To endless questions that become obsessions
Such as how many casualties are acceptable

Would bring their strange conjectures to my mother,
And all their careful estimates and stuff,
For my mom will tolerate a lot of nonsense
But she's also good at when enough's enough.

## Along the Edge of Death

About a mile from downtown walking east
Across the State Street bridge where traffic bends
There lies a cemetery. Or at least
It seems to lie. Perhaps it just pretends.

Perhaps in truth, though feigning otherwise,
It lies awake, at least as wide as me,
Which would explain the winking of the eyes
I seem to see in every solemn tree

And the faint greeting that I seem to hear
When I first enter like an intake of breath
As if . . . but that would be my own I fear.
Breathing is, well, unusual for death

And hardly dignifies with proper gloom
The faded rose of summer, as it were.
As if to warn me there's a tomb
Marked "Rose," a graven name, somebody's sepulchre.

But not for tombstones do I turn aside.
My sorrow's stones are elsewhere. Let them be.
I know nobody here who ever died
Except the one elm. There's always one elm tree.

But my turn here into the cemetery
Has more to do with pine trees than with pain—
Pine trees and cones, maybe a hawthorn berry,
Things I can carry all day in my pocket or brain.

Most berries won't be carried though for long.
You have to pick and eat them right away,
Whether or not the appetite is strong.
"We eat for the hunger that comes," Grandma'd say.

The cemetery lays a feast of greens
And browns and golds—the dressing is the dew —
On shredded sycamore, catalpa beans,
Even the snake that slices the mushrooms through.

For such a feast I hardly know the rules,
What fork to use, whether to pray out loud,
Or pray at all. We must look like such fools
Who pray when God is right here on the ground.

Nevertheless I close my eyes sometimes
And lift my face in something like a prayer
Then taste the air the way you taste fine wines
Pronounce it good, "Vin extraordinaire!"

For here's an alcohol that's flowing free
And first thing in the morning. Every day
Is Pentecost here. Each year Jubilee.
And I a drunk disciple, you might say.

As tipsy as a treetop, half inclined
To stay all day, I linger at the gate.
I wonder if the clientele would mind
If I were, say, a half a season late.

Or if I were to stay all season long
And match myself for pace against the plants;
I think at last I'd learn that gray bird's song
And how the oak leaves do that little dance.

But no, I know, disciples everywhere
Must "Go ye, therefore, into all the world."
My world is in an office in a chair,
And round a telephone my fingers curled.

And I am late already and I know
To go back out the way that I came in
Would take too long, and so I stoop down low
And hold my briefcase tight up to my chin

And take the near way through a little hole
Somebody cut once in the wire fence.
Whoever it was had more than me of soul
And more extravagance or common sense.

One time, I don't know really what I did,
I bent to leave and something came unwound,
And I went flying like a little kid
Hands out in front, my briefcase on the ground,

And as I stood up on the other side
And looked around expecting hoots and jeers,
A man out walking, not one smile belied,
Said, "That hole's been there goin' on fifty years."

And that was all, and then he went away
And left me there till I had caught my breath
Thinking of fifty years of souls who play
Like I do now along the edge of death.

**Inside Myself**

Inside myself, I reach,
Pulling my soul to the surface,
Tearing it open and running my fingers along the inside
To see if the content
Is really just tears.

## Leave-Taking

In fall when black oak leaves and sycamore
Line the wide sidewalk where I walk to work,
I like to look to where they've fallen from.
I look up, lean way back. There they all cling
Deciding when and where and how to drop.
Sometimes I stand a while watching one leaf
I think is ripe for letting go the tree.
I fix on one I think looks kind of tired
The way a child looks fighting sleep whose eyes
Droop long before she'll give her tiny hand
Into her father's to be led to bed.
I think perhaps she'll honor me to see
The moment when the letting go occurs.
God knows I wouldn't tell a soul. I'd keep
Her secret like I'd keep my own if she
Would trust me. I know I could keep still
When it comes to leaves. Role models are so
Few and far between for letting go.
Sometimes I stand quite close to a low branch
Or even touch some brown leaves slightly
To see if I can figure when they'll plunge.
But what I really want to know is how
They go so graciously when done, like one
Relinquishes a handshake at the door
When talk runs out and all the tea is gone.
Leaves look so fine the way they say farewell.
A heart-shaped scar the only sign of pain.
They just drop down—they just drop gently down.
No tears to make an ointment for a grave.

Surrender is all, they would have me know.
And I am nearly taken in each fall.
But I have seen some winters come and go.
And I have loved a little. And I know
There are more ways to die, Horatio,
Than fall philosophy has dreamt of.
Not always grace sufficient will supply
The wherewithal to like it when you die.
Some will hang on, past dying, into snow,
Well into winter, even to next year.
For some it takes a great wind from the north.
For those who absolutely won't let go,
It takes the buds of spring to push them out
Like baby teeth. Don't ask me how I know.
I'd rather go the first way though. Truly,
I would prefer it. To give a curtsy in
My brightest dress and laugh as it swelled out
Like a balloon. Of course, we'll have to see.
I'd rather. But it comforts me to know
That if I get all crazy at the end
And make a scene, I'm still within the realm
Of natural things who also sometimes cling.

## When the Day is Done

Sometimes all day I think of where
    I'll go when the day is done.
Most creatures have a hole where they
    can run when they have to run,
Where it's dry and dark and quiet and
    there's nothing to fear or blame
Or to be brave for, just a hole with a floor
    and some sky with a tunnel for frame.

There's one I know who never goes out
    except to the corner store.
She has an illness, I believe,
    called agoraphobia or
A fear of open spaces, or
    maybe just face to faces,
But she's the sweetest voice you'll ever
    meet on a telephone basis.

On the other hand, there's the bumblebee
    who seems to have no fear.
She thrusts herself into touch-me-nots
    all the way up to her rear
Then staggers out and aims her weight
    again, if a little wider,
Until she bumbles into death
    in the form of a garden spider.

Fear has little to do with size it seems
    and more to do with species
Or with the degree of risk a particular
    woman or bumblebee sees,
Or doesn't see, as the case may be;
    sometimes blinder desires take over,
And it's all you can do to remember your fear,
    so intense is the odor of clover.

Once or twice in my life, I have girded my wits
    and asserted them strenuously
Toward something I wanted and wouldn't have got
    had I sought it more tenuously.
Risk was easier then, for that was when
    I hadn't yet grown tired
Or begun to be encumbered by
    the leavings I'd acquired.

Now they weigh me down here under the ground
    at the base of the willow tree
At the end of the day. But the recluse spiders
    keep an eye on me.
And I on them. I'm not yet ready
    to stay down here for good.
Though when those boughs caress the ground,
    I almost think I could.

## Part of Everywhere

Lean heavily, spirit.

Feel the weight
Your wings belie.
Don't be wary.
Don't beware.
But nestle into nothing
Like a lover.
Yield to air.

Though godlessness is near and silent,
So's God.
Believe it fair.
And lean.
Don't fight
In flight.

If to transcend
Requires height,
Descend
And leave it there.

Downwards is still part of everywhere.

# Credits

*The following poems by Chris Longenecker have been previously published, sometimes with different titles or slight variations. Titles not in parentheses are also used in this book; titles in parentheses are those used in a given publication.*

"For Balance," ("For Sheer Desire"), *Christian Living*, 1988.

"Leave-Taking," *Apprise: South Central Pennsylvania's Regional Magazine*, January 1992.

"This May be Madness" ("Which Dreams"), p. 5; "For Balance," p. 53; "Loon Landing" ("To a Loon"), p. 57; "Not What You Might Think," p. 49; *The Gathering* (Community Mennonite Church, Lancaster, Pa: Parrot Press, 1999).

"Leave-taking," *Season's Plus* (bi-monthly newspaper supplement of *Daily News Record*), November 8, 2002, p. 4

"Just Another Season," *Atlanta Review* 12.1, Fall/Winter 2005, pp. 58-59.

"Some Outside Help," annual Epiphany card of Lancaster Theological Seminary, January, 2006.

## Acknowledgements

I wouldn't write poetry (and probably couldn't) if it weren't for my parents who read and recited poetry to me and listened to me as I was growing up (and even now) and for my brothers and a sister who took (and still take) me seriously, but not too seriously.

I am also blessed to have a husband whose honesty and humor keeps encouraging me even though he never knows when a poetry recitation is going to break out. My extended family has been incredibly supportive as well as other extended families, especially Anne Sensenig's.

Then there are the teachers I was privileged to have who not only introduced me to great poetry but encouraged me to memorize and perform it from that first fourth-grade botched attempt at Ogden Nash to Christopher Dock Mennonite High School's spring forensics competitions, to Eastern Mennonite College where, in some classes, I was given equal credit for poetry recitation as for research. "Every poem is a feat of performance," Robert Frost said, and my teachers took that seriously.

My thanks also go to my community of friends, my women's group, the theater friends, the church friends, and the friends who cross all boundaries and categories, even the ones that were so long in the past they may not know I still think of them and sometimes write a line (or a whole poem) for them.

And I offer a special thank you to John Ruth for inspiring me in the fine art of storytelling and then more recently for believing in my style, sharing my poems with Roma and others, and urging me on to publication.

# The Author

Christine (Chris) Longenecker was born in 1960 in Harrisburg, Pennsylvania, where her parents pastored a small urban Mennonite church. She and her three siblings moved with their parents many times (to Virginia, Oregon, and back to Pennsylvania) before she began attending Christopher Dock High School in Lansdale, Pennsylvania.

After attaining a BA in English from Eastern Mennonite College in Virginia, Chris moved to Washington, DC, where she lived, worked, and volunteered in local theaters for the next five years.

In 1986 she returned to Pennsylvania, this time to Lancaster County, the county of her mother's roots. Here she had planned to teach English, but eventually found more fulfillment working for nonprofit agencies that assisted immigrants and refugees. She worked in this field for the next seventeen years as a legal counselor and resettlement caseworker. She also found a welcome in the Lancaster theater community where she has been involved, primarily with Theater of the Seventh Sister, since 1988.

Eventually her interest in the natural world (and the closure of the program in which she was working) led her to take courses at Longwood Gardens and to pursue a career in gardening. She is now a horticultural assistant at Conestoga House and Gardens.

Chris lives with her husband, Rick Shoup, in a house on the edge of Lancaster city with their cat, Tommy Boy, and many trees. They attend Community Mennonite Church of Lancaster and continue volunteer involvement in theater, a bike club, and with a local arboretum. They also perform programs of Robert Frost poetry together whenever possible.

CPSIA information can be obtained at www.ICGtesting.com
Printed in the USA
BVOW05s1645310815

415076BV00001B/5/P

9 781931 038874